Making Parish Meetings WORK

- PLANNING
- LEADING
- LISTENING
- RUNNING
- EVALUATING

Making Parish Meetings WORK

MEDARD LAZ

AVE MARIA PRESS
Notre Dame, Indiana 46556

Medard Laz is a parish priest in the Archdiocese of Chicago and the founding pastor of Holy Family Parish in Inverness, Illinois, where he served from 1984 to 1995. Father Laz is the author of seven booklets including *Helps for The Separated and Divorced* and *Helps for The Widowed* (Liguori Publications) and the book *Love Adds A Little*  *Chocolate* (Servant Publications). He is also the co-founder of the world-wide program for children of the divorced, Rainbows for God's Children.

© 1997 by Ave Maria Press, Inc.

International Standard Book Number: 0-87793-597-1
Library of Congress Catalog Card Number: 96-52317
Cover design by Elizabeth J. French
Printed and bound in the United States of America.

Library of Congress Cataloging-in-Publication Data

Laz, Medard.
         Making parish meetings work / Medard Laz.
             p.   cm.
         Includes bibliographical references.
         ISBN 0-87793-597-1
         1. Church meetings.   I. Title.
    BV652.15.L39   1997
    254'.6—dc21
    96-52317
                                               CIP

*To the many wonderful people
who have held my hand,
touched my heart, and
guided me through
a lifetime of meetings.*

Contents

INTRODUCTION

Since the Second Vatican Council (1962-1965), one of the most dramatic changes in the Catholic Church has been the rise and the multiplication of meetings. Hundreds of thousands of Catholics now attend regularly scheduled meetings ranging from staff meetings to diocesan planning meetings.

Before Vatican II a certain organizational illiteracy existed in our local churches. Parishes had no parish councils, school boards were rare, and organizations were limited to groups like the Altar and Rosary Society for women and the Holy Name Society for men. Vatican II brought a whole new dimension into the church by reminding us the church is the "people of God." The entire second chapter of Vatican II's Constitution on the Church, also referred to as *Lumen Gentium* (Light of All Nations), is devoted to this description of the church as the new people of God. It illuminates a scriptural image that emphasizes the human and the communal nature of the church rather than its hierarchical and institutional dimensions.

In the initial years after Vatican II, there was an excitement about organized councils and boards due to a sense of a newly found freedom and a desire by the laity to participate in church life. This has long since eroded and given way to an enduring amount of frustration. So often we hear comments like, "Not another meeting to attend!" and "Three hours we've been here. Nothing has been decided. Little has been accomplished. What a waste of time!"

All who are baptized are members of a faith community. They all share in the threefold ministry of Jesus as priest, prophet, and king. This threefold designation brings with it a responsibility and a privilege—to share the revealing and saving Word of God, to partake in mediating responsibilities between God and people, and to participate in leadership responsibilities within the church. The laity and the ordained are not segregated from each other. Nor are they stratified in layers of a holy pyramid, the pope being at the top and the laity at the bottom with dignity and responsibility parceled out according to one's rank on the pyramid. As a result of the Constitution on the Church, intersecting circles are used instead of pyramids to describe the emerging organizational structures throughout the church. As baptized people of God, regardless of being ordained or lay, each person is called to service—though not necessarily to the same type of service—due to one's baptism in Christ:

> For their sacred pastors know how much the laity contribute to the welfare of the entire church. Pastors also know that they themselves were not meant by Christ to shoulder alone the entire saving mission of the church toward the world. On the contrary, they understand that it is their noble duty so to shepherd the faithful and to recognize their services and charismatic gifts that all according to their proper roles may cooperate in this common undertaking with one heart.
>
> *(Constitution on the Church, 30)*

The involvement of the laity in the church is not simply a participation in what may properly belong to the bishops and the priests. Nor is the ministry of the laity a stop-gap measure due to the shortage of ordained priests. The bishops at the Second Vatican Council said that ministry and involvement belong to the laity by virtue of their initiation through the sacraments of baptism, confirmation, and the eucharist.

> (Laity and pastors) are bound together by a mutual need. Pastors of the church, following the example of the Lord, should minister to one another and to the faithful. The faithful in their turn should enthusiastically lend their cooperative assistance to their pastors and teachers.
>
> *(Constitution on the Church, 32)*

Almost all of the people who are employed by the church in an administrative capacity spend many hours per week attending meetings. Yet how many of them, or the others who attend with them, were ever trained in running or participating in meetings? The attitude of many is that meetings are a necessary evil, a part of getting involved in parish or diocesan activities. At the parish and the diocesan level little attention has been paid to making meetings work. Yet they can work!

Robert G. Howes in his book, *Parish Planning, a Practical Guide to Shared Responsibility*, reflects on the parish experience and invokes three cardinal principles that point to the need for parish meetings that work:

1) No parish is an organization, but every parish has an organization.

Parishes and everyone/everything in them are subject to "the human condition." We may not think of a parish as an organization, but it certainly must have an organization. In order to manage a parish and all that goes on in its life, meetings are necessary. We also need to remind ourselves that those who participate at every parish meeting are fallible and finite human beings. The church has always been a mixture of the human and the divine. It is part of the divine mystery enfleshed and incarnated in human persons who are fallible.

2) Participation and planning are two sides of the same pastoral coin.

Put otherwise, when one is crippled, the other limps. Without participation and planning there is fragmentation, a lack of wholeness, and a lack of vision, cohesion, and direction. The parish winds up doing many things poorly instead of a few things well. The result is not planning and participation, but chaos. Board and committee meetings are necessary to plan and to coordinate the major events within a parish. If participation is poor, then the planning is poor, and vice versa. Planning is a skill. It takes vision, effort, and fortitude.

3) Effectiveness = performance + satisfaction.

A parish is effective when it does more things efficiently and when more of its people feel involved and fulfilled in the process. Thus, both in the way it shares and in the way it plans, a parish must at once perform and satisfy.

People look to the parish to fulfill certain needs. Ministries and organizations are called upon to foster personal and spiritual growth for individuals and for the community as a whole. Well-run meetings are a means of instilling a sense of direction and purpose to that which is important in the life of a parish.

Parishioners who share in the leadership role by serving on boards and committees commit themselves to the shared goals of the parish. By working on these shared goals, a sense of ownership is produced. This leads to an increase of interest, pride, and participation in the broader parish community. The parish becomes "family" as individuals get to know and enjoy each other, as friendships are formed and nourished during and after the meetings.

It takes skill and know-how to facilitate a productive meeting as well as skill and personal resources to serve effectively on a board or a committee. For many people it will be the first time they have served on a board or a committee. And even those who are experienced with meetings often find that parish meetings drag on, nothing seems to get accomplished, and polarities materialize. Progress is slow.

We have come to realize that parish or diocesan meetings are often quite different from business meetings or local community meetings. The church is not democratic in its structure, though its meetings can be. And there is a unique bonding and blending that only occurs in a parish setting. There may be heated and even violent disagreements at a meeting between a pastor and his parishioners or among parishioners. And yet, the following Sunday, they all gather around the beautiful and healing table of the Lord.

What goes on at meetings, how meetings are run or not run, and what is communicated as a result of meetings is vital to the health and well-being of the parish, the diocese, and the church.

In the chapters ahead we will look at the governance model that is present in the American church today before we focus on the meetings themselves. At times in the managing of a complex church, there are conflicts that arise between the pastor and a board or a group. In CHAPTER ONE we will consider how these conflicts can be resolved through a process called "democracy of means" so that meetings might be more productive and rewarding.

In CHAPTER TWO we will examine all the work that goes into preparing a meeting; for example, planning an agenda and arranging the meeting space. We will delve into the various elements needed for success as well as factors that lead to frustration, even disaster, and how they can be avoided or at least mitigated. We'll also share some thoughts on when a meeting should be canceled.

CHAPTER THREE focuses on decision-making. Five methods will be detailed with emphasis on the most common method, developing consensus.

In CHAPTER FOUR we will look at ways to evaluate the meeting from a number of perspectives so as to enable productive follow-up.

In CHAPTER FIVE a variety of leadership skills are highlighted, especially those that deal with being an understanding listener.

Some final notes in CHAPTER SIX are provided to allow those who participate in meetings to become more active and to enjoy the tremendous energy that can be generated from productive meetings.

This handbook will be useful to those who participate in a countless variety of meetings at the parish level: the parish staff, pastoral council, school board, religious education board, school staff, committees such as finance and liturgy, and ministry groups such as those for widows, the divorced, seniors, young adults, teens, and many others.

Making Parish Meetings Work is not specifically aimed at general parish meetings such as town hall meetings that are scheduled infrequently and are called to address a specific problem or issue. Elements from this book can be helpful, but this book is directed at regularly scheduled meetings that take place weekly or monthly.

This book will also be helpful at deanery, cluster, vicariate, and diocesan meetings for priests, deacons, religious, and laity. Participants can benefit by taking an in-depth look at the goals and the structures that need to be in place for such meetings. Primarily, however, the focus is on meetings that occur at the parish level.

Making Parish Meetings Work is meant to be a basic guidebook. It is not "the" way to conduct a meeting, but offers many ideas and tools that have proven successful in achieving productive and fulfilling meetings. It focuses on the tasks and content for conducting successful meetings. It does not address relationships or the many dynamics that operate within a group. It does not attempt, for example, to deal with conflict resolution in any in-depth manner. Such items would constitute quite a different book.

Countless hours are devoted to meetings everyday by so many who labor for the church on a professional or a volunteer basis. The aim of this book is to have those people feel that the meetings they attend are productive. Or, if they feel otherwise, *Making Parish Meetings Work* will help them know the reason why and what can be done about it.

One

Leading Your Meetings

The church has survived for two thousand years without the multiplicity of boards, committees, councils, and all the meetings we have today. Why is there another meeting every time we turn around? Are they really necessary?

We have all heard, said, and felt these words many times in the course of our ministry within the church. Someone has remarked, "The church is a very simple structure, when you come right down to it. It only starts to get complicated when you involve people!" But, of course, that's what the church is: people—people involved in its leadership and in its mission.

A Leadership That Is Shared

The Second Vatican Council invited the laity to become leaders within the church and to offer its advice and counsel to pastors and bishops. In 1983, Canon 129 of the Code of Canon Law designated this ministry of leadership to both the ordained clergy and lay persons in the parish as follows:

> 1. In accord with the prescriptions of law, those who have received sacred orders are capable of the power of governance, which exists in the church by divine institution and is also called the power of jurisdiction.

> 2. Lay members of the Christian faithful can cooperate in the exercise of this power in accord with the norm of law.

Diocesan and parish councils as well as school boards, finance committees, and many other committees have developed at the local level in the church in the intervening years. What has happened in the Catholic Church is the creation of a governance model based on the secular experience. Nominations and elections of members and officers are held and meeting procedures are utilized similar to what occurs in the government or business communities. Leadership may take the form of an advisory or a governing board. Pastoral councils, education boards, finance committees, along with women's and men's clubs have constitutions and by-laws that have presidents, vice-presidents, secretaries, and treasurers. Members vote on issues with the pastor having the power of a veto. In some dioceses, the pastor's veto can be appealed to a vicar, a dean, or the bishop. It is not surprising that this new model of lay involvement, leadership, and decision-making has brought with it a host of problems.

The Heart of the Problem

When problems and difficulties do arise on a board or a committee, they are usually connected with three areas: 1) structure; 2) information; and 3) people.

If the problem is with the structure, then the constitution, the by-laws, and the operating procedures need to be examined. A particular board or committee may overstep its boundaries on a particular matter. For example, the finance committee often reports directly to the pastor by virtue of diocesan guidelines. This procedure may cause consternation with members of the pastoral council or the school board when funds are to be raised or allocated.

Problems also arise over how *information* is communicated to members. So often this has to do with an ignorance about roles, responsibilities, and relationships of board and committee members, hired staff, and volunteers. Roles, responsibilities, and relationships are frequently presumed and not written down. Even the best job descriptions only present a partial picture of what is expected of a particular individual.

The continual turnover of staff, volunteers, and board and committee members allows many tasks to fall through the cracks. Many times this is highlighted with the maintenance personnel. Who was expected to set-up the tables and the chairs and to do the clean-up after a meeting or class? How and when was such a set-up or clean-up requested? What set-up or clean-up is a group or committee expected to do itself? Spelling out roles, responsibilities, and relationships in a parish is a challenging task.

The problem may also lie with *the people* who are involved. Certain individuals may understand the structures that are in place and also the roles, responsibilities, and relationships involved, but some may choose not to cooperate. An individual in a leadership capacity might think he or she is above the procedures and fail to sign up for a meeting room or see that it is set up beforehand. Such a person might also schedule meetings at a time when it is inconvenient or impossible for most people to attend.

At times it is difficult to identify or pinpoint the real issue or problem. For example, someone may challenge serving alcohol at a parish function. The chairperson may identify the problem as a structural one and seek out the diocesan guidelines that deal with the issue. The problem, however, may not be structural at all. It may be wrapped up with the people and the personalities involved. There may be a strong bias against alcohol by an individual or a special interest group. It is important to focus on the real problem in a gentle and delicate manner.

Another example could involve a liturgy committee that has begun to discuss the purchase of a new hymnal to be placed in the pews. Without consulting members of the committee, the pastor on his own authority goes ahead and orders a hymnal he prefers. Such examples lead to conflict between the pastor and various committees in the parish. Needless to say, examples like this happen all too frequently.

Who has the authority in such matters? Are we dealing with a people problem, namely, the pastor who has an autocratic style and does not work well with committees? Or is it an informational problem because various committees may not understand their role and their relationship to the pastor? Nevertheless, the end result is a power conflict.

A Democracy of Means

It is important to consider this potential area of conflict before we delve into the specifics of the meetings themselves. The pastor has the ultimate authority in a parish and the veto power to go along with it. Yet the laity is anxious to act in a leadership capacity exercising its talent and ability to help the church. Is there an effective way of dealing with this potential dilemma?

In *Parish Planning*, Howes writes of the hierarchical church: "Advisory committees propose, pastors and staffs dispose." Howes suggests that in the church in America we have a "near democracy." By serving on boards and committees, the laity meets, deliberates, recommends, and sometimes votes. But the pastor retains the ultimate authority resulting in a "near democracy." And with anything "near," like near beer or near authenticity, it is not quite satisfactory. People who have given their time, energy, and talent usually feel put down when they are told "You are only advisory. I decide around here." Even though the pastor is the ultimate authority, few causes are served when his authority is communicated this bluntly.

Howes also speaks of people wanting "substance and results" when they meet. After going through the long process of meeting and recommending a course of action only to find that nothing is done or the pastor has gone ahead and done what he wanted to do, people are frustrated.

They believe they have wasted their time. Their meeting did not yield the result they intended.

Howes says there is a way of defusing this dilemma. He calls it a "democracy of means." For this to occur a pastor must first of all have an appropriate consultation on a given issue or problem. He cannot be operating alone or in a vacuum. The pastor decides and announces the intent or the goal based on the consultation that he has in mind. Then within the constraints of feasibility and orthodoxy, the parish council, the staff, or other committees decide the best means or objectives for accomplishing this goal.

Howes cites contemporary management theories to make his point. In *Parish Planning* he notes that "Planning for a future is not making a blueprint for absolute adherence. It is choosing a direction." He also points to what is called a "solution space" method. "The manager's job is to establish the boundaries around a fairly broad solution space. The individual's responsibility is to find the best way of doing things within that space."

Howes then elaborates on how a parish can specifically implement its democracy of means:

1. The pastor with a consensus from the council or a committee announces a parochial goal; for instance, an outreach program to parishioners who are registered but who do not attend church with any frequency.

2. How to accomplish such a goal becomes the responsibility of relevant persons and committees

within the parish. Mailings, home visits, and get-togethers may be some of the methods and approaches that are chosen over a certain time period. The council, the board, or the committee decide the details.

3. The pastor and the staff may intervene at times with suggestions, but the decisions rest with the persons or the committees who are involved. Two conditions are important:

3.1 The proposed actions and resource comments must fall within the current or anticipated capacity of the parish;

3.2 The proposed actions must be consonant with diocesan and larger ecclesial directives in the subject area.

4. Thus the talents and the energies of a council, a board, or a committee are fully marshaled and respected. The pastor has proclaimed the goal, and together with the laity, decisions are made for carrying out this goal.

Not all conflicts can be resolved through the democracy of means. But such a process will lessen frustrations like those in the example of the pastor buying the hymnals on his own authority. Where the pastor focuses on the intent or the goal that he has in mind, and leaves most of the other decisions up to the council, the board, or the committee, frustration is avoided.

In summary, structural problems can be dealt with by revising constitutions, by-laws, and guidelines.

Informational problems can be handled by informing committee members about the basics of their roles, responsibilities, relationships, and operating procedures. People problems can be managed by using conflict management techniques (some of which are found throughout this book) to facilitate both process and progress. And the use of a democracy of means can sanction a democracy for the laity and a means for the pastor.

Managing a Complex Church Through Meetings

Parishes and dioceses today are very complex and multifaceted. Anywhere from twenty to one hundred different ministries or groups within a parish attract a significant number of parishioners. Often there is a parochial school with hundreds of children, teachers, and volunteers as well as a religious education program for children in public schools. The preparation and the conferring of the sacraments involves hundreds of people, most of them lay. And the maintenance of the physical plant is both costly and time consuming. What must be organized and managed at the parish level is multiplied a hundredfold or more at the diocesan level.

It is impossible for an individual bishop, pastor, principal, priest, religious, deacon, or lay person to effectively manage such activities alone or to make decisions without the broad range of expertise and knowledge that others can offer. Each person has a particularly crucial piece of information about a decision that needs to be made. Jointly and together they represent the sum total of the components necessary to not only make a decision, but to make a good decision. Ours is a complex church and a committee church, whether we like it or not.

By serving on boards, committees, and councils, average parishioners take ownership of their parish or diocese. By becoming an integral part of the decision-making process, an individual Catholic gives flesh and blood to the teachings of the Second Vatican Council that proclaimed that the people are the church. Being involved with the decision-making process of the church is truly a ministry, one through which all of the other good works and ministries can function effectively. The aim is for the parishioner to envision and embrace the parish as "my" parish and the diocese as "my" diocese. The means to this end is not simply involvement, but involvement that is seen as shared ministry. This enables the church to move beyond a "do-for" mentality to a "do-with" form of ministry.

Almost all of us will serve on boards, committees, or task forces at some time. Many of us will be called on to perform specific roles, either to lead in some way or to be a participant. Thus, we need to know how to influence the process from a participant's point of view as well as from a leadership position. The focus here will be on the "before and after" of the meeting as well as the meeting itself. Putting all these pieces together allows us to do the job well.

Boards and committees exist to make decisions and/or assist those in authority to make decisions. In so doing the quality of parish or diocesan life is enhanced. A variety of people with differing backgrounds come together to decide about and to plan for a parish mission, a rescheduling of Mass times, or an outreach program for the unchurched. Effective committees serve as vehicles through which preferences can be expressed. Votes are taken as the group struggles with and moves toward consensus. Leaders, members, and participants speak for themselves and for various groups within the parish. Often this is helpful, sometimes it is not. If a sound structure for the board, the committee, and the meeting itself is in place, generally, a sound decision can be made.

What Meetings Deal With

Various boards, committees, and groups have different objectives at different times. This carries over to the type of meeting structure that is necessary. For example, a pastoral council may need information about the cost of paving the church parking lot. It may want feedback from the parishioners about Holy Week services. The council may want to use some creativity in brainstorming about the type of parish mission that will be planned for Lent. The council might need to set up a time for team-building and goal-setting. It may have to do some decision-making about whether or not to proceed with plans for a new parish center. And the parish council may have to do some problem-solving in order to resolve the dilemma of dozens of people who stand in the back of church each week at Mass and crowd the vestibule. All of this is, of course, far more than a pastoral council could handle at a given meeting. But it provides an example of the kinds of matters that parish meetings deal with, the what of a meeting.

It is essential for every board and committee to know exactly what it is dealing with when it meets. Very often this is not clear. Has this group of people been brought together to seek information or to offer feedback or to share creative ideas? Do they need or want to spend time in team-building? Or do they need to be involved with decision-making and problem-solving? The example of the pastoral council indicates that it is expected and empowered to do all six of these.

It is most important to know what a given board, committee, or group is brought together to accomplish. This should be made clear at the outset by virtue of a mission and/or vision statement. A cluster group of laity may meet monthly to share information and news concerning their respective ministries as well as problem-solve some of the issues that are raised. It needs to be clear that it is not a decision-making body or the gatherer of feedback. An ad hoc committee may simply exist to gather feedback about setting up an adult education program. Many problems and difficulties ensue down the line when people are not sure what they have been called together to accomplish.

What Meetings Provide

Information—Provide important data and the necessary facts

Feedback—Receive input on how a proposal or project is going

Creativity—Brainstorm ideas and concepts

Team-Building—Build group unity through sharing and trust

Problem-Solving—Examine what is wrong and propose solutions

Decision-Making—Consider the facts and the criteria and then decide

Let us look with a little more depth at each of these:

Information

Information can be provided in the form of a status report or a briefing. For example, how the finance committee is doing with its task of increasing the weekly offertory collection. This is basically a one-way communication. Other than asking specific questions or seeking feedback, interaction among the participants is discouraged at an information meeting or the segment of the meeting allowed for it. Providing information keeps a group informed and gives flesh and blood to written reports. However, time limits should be placed on the presentation of information at meetings.

Feedback

Feedback is often seen as a time for critiquing. A feedback mechanism should be designed whereby useful and productive feedback can be given without risking a gripe session. It is important to make feedback descriptive rather than evaluative or judgmental. By avoiding evaluative language, you reduce the likelihood of a defensive response. Thus it is better to point toward a deadline for raffle tickets to be put into the mail rather than complain about people not doing their job. In complex parish or diocesan settings it is important to make sure that the receiver of the feedback can do something about what he or she is hearing. Frustration is only increased when the receiver has no control over a situation.

For example, to harp on the fact that many people are leaving Mass early only leads to frustration since this is an age-old and common problem not easily solved. Feedback is most useful when the receiver has asked for it. And checking out the accuracy of one person's feedback is important. Also, raising one's voice is counter-productive. So often the person who speaks out the loudest intimidates others from speaking out and from offering different viewpoints.

Creativity

The creative meeting—or part of a meeting—is one where people can brainstorm ideas and not necessarily offer solutions to problems. It provides an opportunity to discuss ideas that are tied to the visions of what the church, the diocese, parish, or school can really become. It focuses not on the problems at hand or even the immediate solutions, but rather upon the reign of God in concrete terms. "Wouldn't it be great if we could serve coffee, juice, and rolls after all of our masses on Pentecost or during the summer months and foster a sense of hospitality?" Such meetings or portions of meetings put a new pair of glasses on the members to create a vision of Jesus alive and present in their midst. The energy level at such meetings is usually high. Time spent in this fashion can be a great tool for team-building. It is important that everyone present is invited to participate and to contribute.

Team-Building

One of the goals of boards, committees, and groups within the parish and the diocese is to operate via consensus. Consensus does not mean that everyone on the committee agrees with a given issue, but rather each person can still support an issue given the larger picture with which they are dealing. It is very difficult to achieve consensus from a given group on some matters. So it is important for the group to work toward becoming a cohesive unit. Retreats, study days, faith-sharing, prayer sessions, and social get-togethers all help fashion the group into being a unified body.

These events are not a waste of time. Consensus and unity of purpose can only happen when there is a concerted effort by all to promote a climate of trust, respect, openness, sharing, and honesty. The people who constitute the staff, the council, or the committee must be brought to appreciate their interdependency and be able to build on these. When barriers are reduced, life is a whole lot more enjoyable.

Parishioners and paid staff in leadership positions commit themselves to shared parish goals. When goals are shared there is a sense of ownership, and this increases interest, pride, and participation in the parish as a whole. A community spirit is formed as individuals come to know and enjoy one another. Friendships are made and are often nourished as a result of frequent meetings.

Another goal of boards, committees, and groups within the parish is to grow spiritually. To always "get down to business" at a meeting without an opportunity to put the agenda items and the people in attendance into a faith perspective often results in a loss of vision of the bigger picture of what a parish is all about.

One parish is successful in having fifteen minutes of "faith first" time at the beginning of every meeting. Prompted by a short scripture reading or prayer, members of the group are invited to share their own personal faith experiences on a given topic. Not everyone chooses to contribute. But participants remember and treasure this rebonding, community-building time. It answers the question "Why are we really here at this meeting?" The ultimate answer is "to share our faith and to grow spiritually." But it is also important that the fifteen-minute time limit is not exceeded.

Problem-Solving

By problem-solving we mean an in-depth analysis of a particular issue or problem that needs resolution. The key ingredients are the desire or need to make a change. In problem-solving sessions, it is important for all the participants to understand the need for change. Problems may range from the school being very messy or in need of repairs to complaints that few parishioners like the unfamiliar hymns being introduced at the liturgies.

It is important that various sides of an issue are represented. And it is most important that the issues are what is discussed and not the personalities. Problem-solving time must not get into making judgments about others or putting them down in a group or in public. The goal is to come up with a clear statement of the problem, to consider it in a variety of ways, and then offer several solutions. It is often beneficial to frame the problem in the form of a positive question. "What is it that we would like our parish or our school to look like and how can we get to that point?" rather than "Why is the school such a mess?" Or, "How can we encourage people to sing out while offering them a variety of hymns, both new and old?" rather than "Why are we singing these awful hymns at Mass?"

Decision-Making

The decision-making time of a meeting happens when the objectives and the criteria for making the decision have been identified and there is a clear mandate for the board, committee, or group to take some action. The action component sets the decision-making meeting apart from other meetings because it carries with it a degree of risk for all of the members of the group. They are now accountable for their decision. Some issues are relatively easy to decide upon. Others are so loaded with land mines that making a decision is almost impossible.

A final decision may have to be deferred to the bishop, the pastor, or the principal for the simple reason that given the structure of the diocese, the parish, or the school, they are the ones responsible and ultimately accountable for it. Especially with difficult decisions, it is important that the leader make every attempt to obtain the support from the majority of the board or committee. "One-person" decisions will be difficult to promulgate effectively. And if the leader has made up his or her mind before a meeting about a course of action, it is not wise to pretend it will be a decision-making meeting. People will know they are being used and were brought together to rubber stamp what has already been decided. It is better for the leader to call a meeting and to announce the decision.

It is important to note that groups like the parish council, the school board, or the religious education board regularly deal with and act upon issues in six different ways at a given meeting or over the course of time. Therefore it is vital that the leader and the board members carefully look over the agenda of a meeting to ascertain exactly what is being sought on each item—information, feedback, creativity, team-building, problem-solving, or decision-making. This is vital to know as we now consider the preparation needed for a good meeting. The more that is done beforehand, the more productive the meeting will be.

Two

Planning Your Meetings

Nobody was clear about what the objective of the meeting was. What were we supposed to accomplish?

People kept getting off the subject. The meeting ran way too long.

The participants didn't know they were supposed to bring reports to the meeting. There seemed to be a lot of time wasted.

When people are asked why they find meetings frustrating or unproductive, they often respond with comments like the above. But a few hours of preparation and communication beforehand can result in meetings that do work, thereby saving hours of wasted time for a whole group. Everyone coming to a meeting has an important role and must be serious about making meetings more productive and fulfilling.

Throughout the remainder of this book, the words "leader" and "chairperson" will be used interchangeably. The leader or the chairperson of the meeting is the one who has the responsibility and the authority to conduct the meeting as well as all of the "before and after" details that are involved with meetings that work. The leader may be someone who is ordained, a professed religious, or a lay person depending on the circumstances. Also, the words "participant" and "member" will be used interchangeably throughout the book. These are people who are official members of a board or committee. The word "attendee" will be used to refer to someone who is a guest or in the audience and not officially a member of the board or the committee.

The Agenda

In preparing for a meeting, the most important element is the agenda. This is the blueprint for any meeting that is to be more than a gab session or social gathering. It provides everyone with a picture of what the meeting is going to look like and what is expected to happen. Imagine building your home without a blueprint. It would become a chaotic project. Why have a group of people sit and waste their time for hours without an agenda, a blueprint? Everyone's time today is far too valuable.

An agenda has many important functions including:

1. Defining the purpose of the meeting.

2. Forcing the leader of the meeting to prepare.

3. Helping the participants prepare.

4. Reducing the anxiety level of those coming to the meeting by stating its purpose and objectives.

5. Informing the members, as well as other interested parties, about how and when the board, commitee, or council conducts its business.

6. Providing a useful tool to control the meeting, especially in controlling the use of time.

7. Relating the purpose of the meeting to the larger mission of the parish, the school, the diocese, and/or the church.

A written agenda should be prepared and circulated to everyone who is coming to the meeting five to seven days beforehand if the group meets monthly, bi-monthly, or quarterly. If it is a weekly meeting, the prepared agenda needs to be circulated two days before the meeting date. There should be little or no leeway on this matter.

Most meetings fail because adequate and timely preparation and distribution of the agenda did not occur. This happens for any number of reasons. Often agendas are put together the night before the meeting so participants have no idea what will be discussed. Sometimes they are even put together at the start of a meeting. How often have you heard the question "Does anyone have anything for our agenda today?" Sometimes topics are listed without any regard for the amount of information needed to consider them intelligently; or topics are distributed in so crude a fashion that members cannot understand what preparation may be needed. Whatever the reason or form it takes, poor preparation will have an adverse affect on your meetings.

The responsibility for developing and sending out the agenda lies with the leader of the meeting. It is his or her responsibility to see that everyone coming is prepared. The first step in planning a meeting is to state its purpose and identify what items people attending want to handle. A good way to do this is to examine the minutes of previous meetings for items that might be coming up and also to ask the participants what issues and topics they have. For regularly held meetings, a secretary should contact the members to ask if they have anything for the agenda and to remind them of the meeting.

Agendas should be written in a clear and inviting way, one that conveys what those who are coming to the meeting need to know. Use action verbs to state the agenda items. This gives a sense of movement and accomplishment to the meeting. It is also helpful to tell the participants what the objective or purpose is for the items that are listed. Here is a sample agenda for a pastoral council meeting:

A Sample Agenda

Item	Purpose	Time/Minutes
Opening prayer	Invoke God's Presence	5
Sharing of faith experiences	Team-Building	15
Review agenda	Information	5
Approve minutes	Decision-Making	5
Arrange a speaker for council's prayer day	Information/ Problem-Solving	10
Planning for the parish's 25th anniversary	Creativity/Brainstorming	20
Reworking the council's mission statement	Feedback/Decision-Making	60
Discussing old business	Feedback	10
Discussing new business	Information	5
Closing prayer	Thankfulness/Blessing	5

Presenting the agenda this way provides both a sense of movement as well as a goal. A participant looking over these items several days before a pastoral council meeting will have a better handle on what will transpire at the meeting. Agendas are limited to one page. Minutes from the previous meeting as well as written reports are included with the agenda when it is distributed.

The Leader's Role

The leader and whoever is assisting her or him prepare for the meeting must early on answer the question, "Why are we having this meeting?" Even regularly scheduled weekly or monthly meetings should be examined this way.

It is also important that the groundwork be done and plans be well thought-out before the meeting. But the leader should not create the impression among the participants that the meeting has been so rigidly pre-planned that they are merely getting together to give their assent. The group needs to feel that their ideas, views, feedback, information, and skills at problem-solving and decision-making are valued and appreciated. They need to feel ownership.

Sorting Out the Topics

It is up to the chairperson to decide what and how many topics can be effectively addressed in any given meeting. This is best determined with the help of officers, associates, or assistants.

Sometimes a meeting may have to focus on a single item because of its importance to the group. Oftentimes unfinished business from previous meetings must also be attended to.

To aid the effectiveness of a meeting, it is advisable whenever possible to keep the agenda topics in the same general subject area, that is, have them related to one another. A number of unrelated topics makes it more difficult for the participants to work effectively. There is a limit to the number of new ideas a group can absorb in a couple of hours. So the number of unrelated topics should be kept at a minimum for one meeting.

In preparing the meeting's agenda, the leader sorts through the various submitted items to see how relevant or important each item is. The leader has a sense of which items are inappropriate for group discussion such as personal, confidential, or personality issues that are better dealt with through one-on-one communication or by another means. At times, items make it to an agenda that should never be there in the first place. For example, "housekeeping" items, such as maintenance and room-scheduling often find their way onto agendas and take up valuable time.

When an item is excluded from the agenda, the individual who proposes it should be notified before the meeting by phone or with a note about why it will not be addressed. This way the one who proposes an item receives the feedback to which they are entitled. The goal here is not to keep items off the agenda, but to consider the best way of handling a variety of items. Most people who are submitting items are usually not aware of what else needs to be handled. When they find out, they might easily agree to handling their item as a report or holding off to another time.

The remaining items usually fall into three categories:

Information
Discussion
Decision

These groupings are important because they allow the various items to be categorized and located on the agenda at appropriate times. Assessing the topics in this manner forces the leader to clarify both the purpose and the direction of the meeting.

The leader also assesses committee or subcommittee reports. Three things are to be noted about the presentation of reports at meetings:

1. Committee or subcommittee reports provide important information about vital areas in the parish, school, or diocese. They are to be presented to duly empowered boards, committees, and councils.

2. With rare exceptions, committee reports are written and included with the agenda when it is sent out. This gives the participants the opportunity to read and review the reports beforehand.

3. Whoever has submitted the report beforehand

can verbally touch on the main points of the report at the meeting and receive feedback and support. If a committee or subcommittee has separate items to report, they should be organized with similar topics when they are presented. A subcommittee report should not bounce back and forth from school maintenance to spiritual development to parking problems.

We have all sat through many long and tedious meetings where reports were not handled in this fashion. With no preliminary written report to consider, the participants and the attendees endure a lengthy presentation, hearing about the subject matter for the first time. They are also unprepared to ask intelligent questions. The majority of a meeting can be taken up with a single report without it even being the main item on the agenda. Distributing completed reports in advance of the meeting is the better way, but it takes planning and discipline.

In checking over the agenda items, the leader may have to see to it that a particular individual is present at the meeting for a worthwhile discussion to take place, or that certain information is available.

The leader may sense that an agenda item is too complex to be handled effectively and efficiently, and it may need to be broken down into more manageable parts. The reverse can also be true. Sometimes there are agenda items that need to be combined because they logically fit together and are best handled as a unit.

As the leader puts the agenda together he or she realizes that meetings are comprised of three parts, a beginning, a middle, and an end. But to emphasize and clarify these in the context of an effective and an efficient parish meeting we use rocket launching terminology to emphasize the three separate time frames.

The Three Periods of the Meeting

Each meeting usually has three distinct segments: the *blast-off;* the *in-orbit;* and the *re-entry* periods.

The *blast-off* period is the beginning of the meeting: the opening prayer, the welcoming of any guests or visitors, the sharing of faith experiences, the review of the upcoming agenda, the handling of preliminary business, as well as approval of the minutes from the previous meeting.

The *in-orbit* segment focuses everyone's attention effectively and efficiently on the most important and the most difficult item or items that need to be handled. It is the crucial part of the meeting where the majority of the energy and time is expended. The goal is to get to this point of the meeting in a reasonably short period of time. In a typical two-hour meeting it is important to be in-orbit within a half hour after starting.

The last part of the meeting is the *re-entry.* After the major business has been dealt with, people can begin to unwind a bit as the intensity lessens. Additional reports, brainstorming, feedback, and old or new business are good topics for this phase.

We have all been at meetings where heavy work items are introduced at this part of the meeting, possibly well after two hours have transpired. Most people's attention has greatly diminished, there is little participation, heads are down, and people are doodling on their papers. Very little can be accomplished. Even if decisions are made at this point, they may come back to haunt the group because they were not well phrased, considered, or voted upon. Such a meeting may well have suffered from a late beginning, a lengthy launching, or an over-loaded agenda. Perhaps the leader did not control the meeting adequately.

A sample agenda with segments

Opening prayer
Sharing of faith experiences   **Blast-off**
Approve minutes

Arrange a speaker for council's
   prayer day
Planning for the
   parish's 25th anniversary   **In-orbit**
Reworking the
   council's mission statement

Discussing old business
Discussing new business   **Re-entry**
Closing prayer

The leader also has to determine who is to attend the meeting. Once the goals and the objectives have been clarified and the agenda put together, it is important to determine who should attend and why it's important for them to be there. People who are responsible for agenda items, those who need to be heard from on the critical issues, and those who can provide additional needed information are to be present. If the funding for a junior high school program is to be discussed, then the junior high coordinator really needs to be present.

The logistics of the time and the place of the meeting are to be clear in the attendees' minds through proper notification and communication. It is vital that they have the agenda, minutes, reports, and other documents that will be discussed at the meeting. This way people do not have to be brought up to speed during the meeting.

The Environment

Another consideration for holding a meeting is the environment. Even though many parishes and schools are short on good meeting space, where the meeting is held and the use and arrangement of tables and chairs has a lot to say about its overall tone and outcome. Even if the meetings must be held in conditions far from ideal, always try to make the most out of what is available. Fortunately there is a trend in parishes to establish and furnish rooms specifically designated as meeting rooms.

The room that is used for the meeting should offer both physical and psychological requirements for comfort and serviceability. Our surroundings do affect the way we think and act, and a poorly arranged or uncomfortable room is not likely to produce positive meeting results. The room should provide privacy and be free of distractions. Windows should be draped or the chairs should face away from them.

Tables are essential and chairs should be comfortable and not crowded together. They are best arranged in such a way as to meet the desired degree of participation. People taking part need to be able to see each other eye-to-eye. The ten- and twelve-foot tables that parishes are so famous for, can be arranged in a rectangle, a square, or a triangle so that eye contact is made. If there is to be an audience or guests present, a U-shaped arrangement facing the audience is preferable to a straight line of tables looking out at them. It is best to access the seating from the rear of the room so that as the audience comes and goes, the meeting is not continually being disturbed.

The lighting should be soft but sufficient for note-taking. It may need to be regulated for showing slides and overhead transparencies. The meeting is best held in a place where there is accessibility to overhead projectors, flip-charts, stands, blackboards, TV's, and VCR's.

Ventilation is also important. In a two-hour meeting a room can easily become stale and over-heated. To be able to open a window or a door to get fresh air circulating yet still maintain privacy is sometimes an accomplishment.

Refreshments set a welcoming and inviting tone for a meeting. With the tight schedules that many people have today, some parishes are providing more than just coffee and juice at meetings. Because people rush to and from work in order to make a meeting, rolls in the morning or finger sandwiches in the evening may be appropriate. The type of refreshments to be served can be discussed and the members can take turns in helping to provide them.

When *Not* to Meet

One final note about meeting preparation. It is important to understand when not to have a meeting. Here are some of the many good reasons for canceling or rescheduling a meeting:

1. The subject matter could be addressed more effectively in some other way.

2. The timing is not right.

3. The key participants are not available.

4. There will not be a quorum present.

5. There is inadequate data or time to prepare.

6. The central issue is confidential (e.g., personnel issues) and it cannot be fully shared with the participants.

7. The leader or the one in charge has made up his or her mind on the central issue.

8. The leader who is key to the matters at hand cannot attend.

9. There is not enough business to warrant a meeting.

10. There is too much hostility in the group and until this is dealt with and people have had a chance to calm down, such a meeting would do more harm than good.

Three

Running Your Meetings

The leader who has done a good job preparing will walk into the meeting room feeling good about what is to happen because she or he has a plan of action in mind. The meeting leader who is confident about the proceedings will be noticed by everyone in the room.

Starting on Time

At the top of everyone's list of what needs to be improved with meetings is starting them on time. We have all entered a meeting room hoping to begin only to discover that a number of participants are not present. Then the leader suggests that we wait a few minutes until everyone has arrived. Another fifteen or twenty minutes go by as the latecomers straggle in. Meanwhile, those who were already in the room, go to the washroom or to get a cup of coffee. Others get into side conversations and the start of the meeting is delayed even further.

Starting late disrespects those who arrive on time and is unconsciously supportive of those who come late. "Starting late becomes the norm, so why arrive on time?" they reason. Waiting for habitual latecomers is not likely to cure them of their habit.

Handling the Tardy Member

The leader has the authority and the responsibility to begin the meeting on time. Starting without latecomers may make them sufficiently conspicuous so that the next time they may not be late. Those who have made the effort to arrive on time will respect the leader for consistently beginning on time.

If group members continue to arrive late and there is little or no purpose in beginning the meeting without them, the leader needs to meet privately with the tardy members and stress why arriving and starting on time is necessary.

If the tardiness is a result of a scheduling difficulty, then the leader needs to consider changing the time or the day of the meeting. Any proposed scheduling change is then put before the whole group to decide. Sometimes an encounter such as this forces a committee member to come to grips with the reason for being tardy. For example, the root of the tardiness may be that he or she is over-committed in their life and must pare down some involvements.

Some parish groups have difficulty with clergy or religious consistently coming late to a meeting. Dealing with this should not be avoided. Clergy and religious cannot assume privileges of tardiness. If the clergy or the religious are leading the meeting, it is their responsibility to begin on time. If they are participants or attendees and there is a reason for their absence, the leader should be aware of this and mention to the others at the beginning of the meeting that Father or Sister had a wake or another commitment and will be coming later.

Setting the Tone

The leader sets the tone of the meeting in the first few minutes. The opening remarks set the climate of what is to follow. These remarks tend to be positive or negative. They can stimulate people to want to participate or move them to withdraw from participation. The good leader always tries to open the meeting on a positive note, even if the occasion hardly calls for optimism.

The following is a list of qualities the leader should endeavor to display:

- Enthusiam
- Interest
- Openness
- Sincerity
- Straightforwardness
- Objectivity
- Calmness
- Balance
- Receptivity
- Hospitality

Each participant should feel welcome, sensing that their presence is valued and that the leader of the meeting is in control of what is about to transpire.

As part of the opening remarks, the leader might say: "I'm delighted to be here with you today." Such a statement relaxes the group and reveals his or her good will. The participants sense the person running the meeting is confident, warm, calm, and in charge.

The leader's opening remarks should avoid a tone that is:

Negative:

"We'd better get started because we're already running late." "It seems we're missing quite a few people." "I wonder if this was a good night for the meeting."

Caustic:

"I don't know why people can't seem to find the right room."

Satirical:

"I'm so happy to see all your smiling and happy faces in front of me today."

Boring:

"Now before we actually begin our meeting there are a few housekeeping chores I need to discuss with you. . . ."

Opening with a Prayer and/or Faith Sharing

Most parish and diocesan meetings begin with a prayer. This is a wonderful opportunity for deepening faith and not something simply to get out of the way.

A member of the group is invited in advance to prepare an opening prayer. The format is almost limitless—a scripture reading and a reflection, a prose or poetry reading, a meditation, a song, a taped reflection, a breathing exercise tied into a meditation, or centering prayer. The opening prayer need not and should not be lengthy. It is best if it fits into the overall subject or tone of the meeting. The prayer can be seasonal. Even if some of the participants feel a bit uneasy with it, the opening prayer might well stretch their faith in any number of ways. Doing something dynamic or meaningful with the opening prayer is also a way to help motivate people to arrive on time.

As was mentioned in the previous chapter, more and more parishes are seeing the need for faith sharing to be included in their meetings. At the outset of a meeting it is a time for rebonding and getting in touch with one another at a deeper faith level. A parish meeting has to be more than strictly business. For this reason, one parish designated this time as a "faith first" period and the fifteen minutes has become sacred time. However, it is limited to fifteen minutes. During this time members are invited to share moments when they felt God's presence in their lives, or share personal stories of faith from everyday life, or relate times when they realized God's love. Some people may feel uneasy doing this the first time or two, but most warm to the practice. No one should ever be forced to participate.

Setting Guidelines and Ground Rules

To work efficiently together and to achieve their purpose, the participants need guidelines and ground rules. These should be prepared in writing and passed out at the group's first meeting where they can be discussed, modified and agreed upon. At the beginning of a new year of meetings or when a number of new members join, the guidelines and ground rules can be passed out, reviewed, and modified. Over the course of a year, the leader may want to open the meeting by highlighting one or two points from the list.

Here is a sample list of possible guidelines and ground rules:

◆ Start and end the meeting on time.

◆ Stick to the agenda and the time frames established.

◆ Don't interrupt when someone else has the floor.

◆ One person speaks at a time with no side discussions.

◆ Everyone's ideas are valuable.

◆ Build on the ideas of others rather than jumping to new ones.

◆ Everyone is encouraged to take notes of key ideas.

◆ Treat others with the respect that you would like for yourself.

◆ Deal with issues and not with personalities.

◆ Don't be repetitive.

◆ Be brief in your remarks.

◆ Everyone participates, no one dominates.

◆ Remain open-minded and non-judgmental.

◆ Stress confidentiality concerning the various topics to be discussed.

◆ Complaints are welcome when they are accompanied by a suggested solution.

◆ The leader is empowered to enforce the guidelines and the ground rules.

Guidelines and ground rules are of great advantage to making parish meetings work. These "process ground rules" set the stage. They let those in attendance know:

◆ How the leader wants to have the meeting run or managed.

◆ That the time everyone is devoting to the meeting is important and the one in charge is carefully considering the use of time.

◆ That the leader of the meeting is in control.

It is also a good idea for the participants to take notes, a technique that has been shown to improve listening. Taking notes is a more active listening process than simply sitting and hearing passively what is going on. Participants will get more from the discussion when they jot down their own thoughts as well as any new data that is put forth.

The leader of the meeting quickly reviews the agenda. Additional copies should be available for those who did not bring their own and for any other participants or guests. Changes to the agenda should be noted. Next to the items listed along with the action to be taken, time allotments are given. This places a relative importance on each item and lets the participants know where the meeting is heading. Adjustments can be made as the meeting moves along. The leader can also announce who will be addressing each of the agenda items. All of this will help the leader and the group as a whole ascertain when to move on and where to direct an item or an issue so that the meeting can proceed.

Here is a sample school board agenda that could be reviewed:

Item	Purpose	Time / Minutes	Who
Opening prayer			Tom
Sharing of faith experiences	Team-Building	5	Jean
Review agenda information		5	
Approve minutes	Decision-Making	15	Ed
Reviewing tuition policy	Information /Decision-Making	20	Bob
Planning for pre-school program	Creativity/ Brainstorming	50	Ann
Hiring two new faculty members	Information/ Problem-Solving	20	Sister
Discussing old business	Feedback	5	Ed
Discussing new business	Information	5	
Closing prayer		5	Sue

Reviewing and Taking Minutes

Written minutes are necessary because they provide a clear record of actions taken by participants at a meeting. They capture the key decisions, record how various items were resolved or handled, and help clarify assignments. They also provide a reference and starting point for the next meeting.

Those who could not attend the meeting find minutes most helpful. They help prevent misunderstandings from arising. If possible, it's a good idea to have someone who is not a participant in the meeting record the notes and then prepare the minutes. It is difficult for a board member or a participant to be both the recorder and an active participant in a meeting. The minutes are not a transcript of the meeting. Rather they should contain the following points:

◆ Date and time

◆ Attendees

◆ Agenda topics discussed

◆ Definition of problems

◆ Alternatives presented

◆ Solutions agreed upon

◆ Assignments agreed upon and accepted

◆ Deadlines

◆ Follow-up actions

If minutes are not kept or are poorly done they will adversely impact the effectiveness of the board or group. The more to the point they are, the better. The minutes should be typed, approved by the chairperson, and distributed to the participants within a week after the meeting. If what was discussed and the conclusions reached differ from the group's perception, then adjustments can be made by the group at the next meting.

Individual and/or committee assignments should be reviewed at each meeting even if the task is not completed. The group needs an opportunity to review the progress that is taking place. People often do not follow through after a meeting. Reviewing progress at each meeting is important for successfully completing tasks.

A good time to get a progress report on assignments is while reviewing the minutes of the previous meeting. If more time is required, it can be added to the agenda, or handled under old business. In any case, not much time should be allotted for either getting an update on assignments or reviewing minutes.

Making Announcements

There are always announcements to be made at parish meetings. These can be made at the blast-off or the re-entry part of the meeting. They should be non-controversial in nature, short and to the point, and limited in number. An endless stream of announcements converts the meeting into another parish bulletin or newsletter.

Conducting the Meeting

Here is a thumbnail outline of the points that the leader needs to remember to conduct an effective meeting:

- Start the meeting on time.
- Establish the ground rules and guidelines.
- Follow the agenda.
- Participate as a member of the group.
- Retain the power to stop what is happening and change the format.
- Clarify roles.
- Push for accountability.
- Focus the group on the issues.
- Ensure everyone's participation.
- Regulate the discussion and the time spent on each item.
- Deal with and control problem people.
- Remain neutral during disagreements.
- Complete the meeting on schedule.

The Role of the Chairperson

The leader or the chairperson has the most challenging role in the whole process of making a meeting work. He or she is supposed to develop, crystallize, motivate, or encourage the group to achieve and accomplish the goals set before it.

And since people look for someone to either praise or blame, the participants will attribute both the positive and negative things that happen to the effectiveness of the leader.

Being an effective leader is a complicated task. He or she has to be thinking far enough ahead of the group to point the way it might proceed, as well as offer models of alternate actions for the group's consideration. But the leader cannot be too far ahead or he or she will get beyond the horizon of the business at hand. Each chairperson needs to grow into the position, carefully developing her or his own leadership style.

Before taking on the task of leadership an individual should assess the task much like evaluating a new job. He or she should consider the amount of support and resources that will be available and the amount of time the position will require. It is also vital to take a good look at the history and the nature of the group. What is expected of the committee? How much cohesiveness or division exists?

In choosing a chairperson it is helpful to understand that leaders usually have one of two basic orientations. They may be task-oriented, in which case they will emphasize getting the job done, or they may be people-oriented, in which case they will emphasize relationships. Rarely is someone completely one way or the other. People often fluctuate between one or the other, sometimes intuitively, sometimes intentionally. One is not better than the other.

If you are energized by social contacts you are more likely people-oriented. If you get satisfaction from achieving goals and accomplishing tasks, you are task-oriented.

It is important to remember these orientations when choosing a chairperson. You need to consider the person with the traits most needed by the group. If it is unclear what would be best for the group, let an acting chairperson run the meetings while the dynamics of the group become more apparent.

Such committees as the parish council, the school board, or the men's and women's clubs may in fact include a method of selection of officers in their by-laws. A process of nomination and voting would be detailed along with a set term of office. Although democratic, such methods may risk turning the determination of a leader into a popularity contest. For example, someone with the highest profile through other involvements may be chosen, but may not be a very effective leader in these circumstances.

If a group or a committee is newly forming, there are advantages and disadvantages to the leader being hand-picked or appointed by someone in authority. For example, if the pastor feels that a certain individual possesses many or all of the qualities listed above, then the group is being blessed with someone who can lead them effectively. But if the hand-picked leader is the pastor's mouthpiece and operates in an authoritarian or a weak manner, the group will feel it is a rubber stamp.

A newly forming group may want to meet once or twice before choosing a leader. Some groups try to be democratic to the point of rotating leaders from meeting to meeting. Experience shows that such rotation rarely works.

If the potential chairperson has been a member of the committee or group, then he or she has a good perspective of the requirements of the position. It is still helpful to review all the individual members, assessing their strengths and weaknesses. Do they possess what it will take to get the goals and objectives accomplished? Additions or replacements may be needed.

The Key Idea

The progress of the meeting and of the group is best served when the leader can capture a key idea or central issue that needs to be considered, discussed, and possibly voted on.

Often members of a group will have an emotional response to the key idea or central issue. The chairperson must lead them past this emotional response. That may be best accomplished by providing a new or fresh approach that gets to the heart of what is being discussed or debated.

Here is an example of how a chairperson might capture a key idea:

> We have heard more than a few people voice strong objections to dropping the Sunday 7am Mass. Father John has told us that despite his best efforts, he has not been able to find a priest for this liturgy. He cannot do it himself since he already has three Sunday Masses. We all would like to see the 7am Mass continue, but given the priest shortage, that is not realistic. I suggest we consider changing the 8:30am Mass to 8am to better serve the early risers in the parish.

The leader also provides interpersonal leadership at the meeting. This happens when the leader becomes the cheerleader of the person rather than the idea. "You did an absolutely marvelous job, Herb, in organizing and directing our successful campaign to buy a new organ for the church. What do you think about our prospects for raising money for the parish center?" A very favorable spotlight is cast on Herb and hopefully his ensuing remarks will move the meeting forward to the point where a decision can be made.

A Standard of Behavior

The leader also sets a standard of behavior for the group. If the leader strays from the guidelines and the ground rules, the other members probably will as well. If the leader criticizes others, this will set a tone for others to do the same. If the leader ignores deadlines, then deadlines will become unimportant for the group. The leader or chairperson models the expected behavior of the participants.

Finding the Common Ground

The leader is also called upon to keep the big picture in mind. While other board members can be partisan to their own issues or ideas, the chairperson continually tries to move the group to see and understand the wider implications of an issue. For example, if the group is dealing with the reluctance of some parishioners to have the parish utilize altar girls at Mass, the leader can respond:

> Though some people will take exception to our having altar girls in our parish, don't we have an obligation to the Spirit that is guiding the larger church? There must be a way that we can educate our people to a fuller acceptance of women in new roles in the church.

The leader searches to put issues in context and to find the common ground where the church can come together and move forward.

Delegating Responsibility

Leadership is not a one-person show. In order to move forward, the leader must delegate responsibility to others. The work of the leader is to facilitate the doing of the task, not to do the task alone. Many leaders reach exasperation and say, "I'll do it myself." This is often the result of someone not living up to the standard that the leader expects. Possibly the leader's standard is too high and she or he is asking too much. Checking with someone who is removed from the situation and who can provide an unbiased opinion is often a good idea. A job can get done, but not always in the exact way that the leader would like.

The leader supports, persuades, and encourages the members of the group to take on and to complete the work of the board or the committee. Good leaders are able to nudge those with talents and abilities to accept and complete the tasks as needed. Often this means helping them to get started by meeting with them or calling them after the meeting to map out exactly what needs to be done.

Negative incentive is not a good motivating force. A statement such as, "If someone doesn't step forward, we might as well close our meeting" hardly motivates anyone to an enthusiastic response. Rather, support and nurturing will pay dividends over the long run.

The leader realizes the frustration inherent in his or her job. Not getting members of the group to volunteer or to complete an assignment as agreed upon should not be taken personally.

Treating All Members Equally

Members of the committee or board are seen as equals. All members have an equal right to express their opinion on any issue. Sometimes a member's suggestion may not be helpful, but this does not justify ignoring such an individual. On the other hand, the leader has a responsibility to temper anyone who tends to dominate the meeting. Some people like to hear themselves talk, enjoy the spotlight, or have strong opinions and want to sway everyone else. The participants appreciate when the leader discreetly interrupts and thanks such speakers for their ideas, possibly summing up the central point that has been made. This allows speakers to feel they have been heard and the agenda to move forward.

Drawing out those reluctant to participate is also important. It helps shift focus away from those who monopolize the floor. Often people need to be encouraged to participate. The fact that certain people do not volunteer information does not necessarily mean that they do not have anything to say. Often they have something important to say, but need the chairperson to give them the green light. For example, "Bill, you and I were talking about this issue after Mass last Sunday. Would you share some of your ideas with the group?" It is a good rule of thumb that where there are a dozen or less participants at the meeting, the leader should make sure everyone has been invited to speak at least once in the course of the meeting. The more the leader tempers those who like to dominate at meetings, the easier it will be over the course of time to elicit greater participation, contribution, and ownership from the other members.

Stimulating the Discussion

If the issue under discussion is important, people will jump right in. But most of the time the leader must start the ball rolling. A more general question addressed to the group invites a response: "What do you hope our marriage preparation couples will get out of the sessions we are having with them?" The next question might have to be more specific. "Before you got married, what did you find beneficial with the pre-Cana classes you attended?" At times it is helpful to brief one of the participants in advance to ask certain questions or to raise a given point.

Dealing with Controversies

When controversies ignite, the chairperson needs to step in to prevent the meeting from being torn apart. Sometimes a short recess can be called. Something might be said to lessen the tension or lighten the mood. The chairperson might be able to intervene in the discussion long enough to take it away from the parties involved in the controversy. Sometimes bringing in another participant to speak also allows those who have been arguing an opportunity to cool off.

Getting Through the Agenda Tactfully

The leader keeps each topic or subtopic in its allotted time span, always steering discussion toward the key issues. If the discussion has to be cut short, then the leader can break into it with some relevant point that will tie the speaker's comments into a further statement of understanding or agreement. However, the leader should avoid being a bulldozer. When he or she steps in, it should be for the purpose of building a bridge to a concluding idea or tying up the points that were made while coming to a conclusion. Getting through the agenda is not simply a matter of moving things along or trying to keep to the schedule.

Getting to a Focal Point

Timing is crucial at meetings. The chairperson tries to get all of the relevant points concerning an issue on the table without any one faction dominating the entire discussion. To go on for an hour or more hammering away at a single point makes most of the people in the room uneasy. The need to focus on the key issue or issues is important. Here are six suggestions adapted from Dr. Robert K. Burns' book *Five Listening Techniques,* for capturing the opportune moment at a meeting so as to get to the focal point.

The Approach	What to Say
1. Paraphrase the main idea	"Oh, so you believe that...."
	"Based on what you've said, I see that you want to...."
2. Indicate you understand the feeling behind the idea	"You seem to feel strongly about this."
	"It seemed unfair to you at the time."

The Approach	What to Say
3. Listen without making a value judgment	"Say a little more about that." "Then what happened?"
4. Use the five W's:	
Who?	"Who did you have in mind?"
What?	"What did you think about...?"
When?	"When do you plan to...?"
Where?	"Where did you see this happening?"
Why?	"Why did you comment...?"
5. Find out if all sides of a question have been considered	"Tell me what you like about this." "What is your major concern?"
6. Bring the conversation to a logical break point to see if more discussion is required	"As I understand it, you want to...." "Following up on the initial proposal that you have made...."

The focal point is not always meant to bring an issue to a conclusion, but to help the members of the group see where they are. Then, if necessary, they are prepared for another round of productive discussions. If the focus is missed, particularly by the more vocal members, the group can drift off on tangents.

Leaders must be careful how they interject in order to focus. Their input should never be viewed as an opportunity to advance their own position or to give weight to it. At a certain point the leader can ask, "Now where are we with all of this?" The members need to decide if they can conclude or vote on the matter, continue the discussion, or find a different way of proceeding. The chairperson must find a way of not letting things get out of hand. This means being fair and equitable as well as exercising control.

With poor progression throughout a meeting, the group members will leave wondering what was accomplished, or more likely, they'll leave with false assumptions. It is good for the group members to step in and ask what was decided on an issue or a sub-point before the meeting progresses any further if the chairperson has not done so.

If discussion on a topic has gotten too involved and becomes a threat to keeping the meeting on schedule, the chairperson should exercise his or her authority and interject with an appropriate comment. For example:

> It's after nine o'clock and we've been on this issue for an hour and a half. As you can see from the agenda, we have two more items to get to. I suggest we spend ten more minutes trying to get a consensus on this issue. If we cannot, after the meeting we will have to explore other options for resolving the matter.

If there is agreement on what has been decided and what lies ahead on this issue, the meeting can move on to the next point on the agenda. The summary of what was said will appear in the minutes of the meeting.

A good tool for keeping a meeting on target is called the internal summary. At an appropriate time in a discussion the chairperson can step in and offer a summary so the meeting can move on. Here is what an internal summary at a parish council or a liturgy meeting might sound like:

> I believe I have this in order, but help me to check it over. So far we have generally agreed that we would serve coffee and juice after the 5:00 o'clock Saturday Mass and after the 9:00 o'clock Sunday Mass until Lent begins. This will take place in Rush Hall. It will be sponsored by the women's club who will do the setup and the cleanup as well as provide the refreshments. Mary will be our liaison with the women's club. John will be responsible for publicity in the bulletin, announcements, and flyers. Bill will monitor how it is going from week to week, keeping a count of the numbers, etc. And we will all evaluate the progress at our April meeting. I believe I have everything we talked about.

Not all matters can be settled or decided in a tidy manner. Some meetings can even get unruly. It's the chairperson's job to maintain control without stifling debate or the expression of opinions.

Even in the most difficult meetings, each person needs to walk out of the room feeling they were heard and they were treated fairly. The best run meetings do not preclude someone from feeling upset about how their issue was handled. But if the leader did a good job in running the meeting and handling the personalities and the issues, such experiences will be minimized.

Leaders must exercise their authority carefully. Their primary purpose is to facilitate the attainment of the goals. They need the cooperation of the members of the group to reach those goals. If leaders become authoritarian there will be silence or resistance. A good deal of respect goes with the office of chairperson or the leader of the meeting. But all respect must be earned.

Making the Decision

Few decisions that most councils, committees, boards, and groups are called on to make are clear and simple. When a group reaches a decision, it is making a judgment and choosing among alternatives. Rarely is it a choice between right and wrong. Most decisions are compromises.For example:

◆ A weekday morning Mass is dropped, but a communion service and an evening Mass during Lent are added.

◆ The church will be closed an hour earlier but opened earlier in the morning than before.

◆ There will be one date for First Communions,

but the children will sit with their families and come up and receive communion with them as well.

There are five traditional methods of decision-making common today. All are used on church related meetings. The five are:

The Authoritarian Decision

The Majority Decision

The Minority Decision

The Consensus Decision

The Default Decision

Let's take a look at the pros and cons of each method.

The Authoritarian Decision

This is usually made in a quick, matter-of-fact way by the person in charge or whoever is responsible for managing the situation. Old business, new business, and many other items need to be attended to and decided upon in this way. For example, at the staff meeting it is decided that the pastor's and the business manager's signatures will be on the parish's checks. At the pastoral council meeting the president decides to begin the meeting even though a key person has not yet arrived.

The Pros:

◆ It promotes decisive action when it is needed.

◆ It moves secondary matters along, separating them from the more important ones.

◆ It trusts the leadership qualities of the chair person.

◆ It creates a sense of accomplishment and momentum.

The Cons:

◆ It may mean that some important matters at times are glossed over.

◆ Its overuse will result in a non-participative or a rubber-stamp mentality.

◆ It may result in a tendency to foster too much power in the hands of the leader.

◆ It leads to little or no discussion on certain matters.

The Majority Decision

Voting by a show of hands for a majority decision is used only as a means of demonstrating support and unity on a given proposition or proposal, or as a straw vote to assess people's opinions and attitudes. When a group is strongly divided, deciding via consensus is a more favored course of action (see page 85). A "simple" majority means that one vote more than fifty percent has carried the decision. A "two-thirds" majority means that two-thirds of those voting are necessary to carry or defeat a motion. A group can decide which type of majority it favors in its decision-making. Usually two-thirds is favored for a vote so that decisions are not made by a slim margin.

Majority decisions are appropriate only for issues that will not be divisive or cause anger and bitterness. The majority decision can foster a competitive approach to parish decision-making. It is efficient for handling some matters, but when such a vote causes division and dissension, a sense of trust within the community will be harmed.

An example of the opportunity to use majority decision approach is:

> After a lengthy written committee report and a discussion, there is much support at the meeting for hiring off-duty police on Sundays to help direct traffic. A vote is taken and a majority decision of more than two-thirds favors the proposal.

An example of when *not* to use this approach would be:

> A proposal to raise the tuition for students in the religious education program is made at the education board meeting. The debate is heated and the members of the board are split down the middle. The chairperson chooses instead to handle the matter by a consensus decision.

Majority decision is also used where larger numbers are present and it is important to achieve a sense of democratic participation:

> At a teachers' meeting it is decided by a majority vote that the last person to leave

the teachers' lounge after school is responsible for shutting off the lights and locking the door.

At a lectors' meeting it is decided by a majority vote that the lectionary used for weekends will be kept in the chapel and not in the sacristy.

The Pros:

◆ It is the democratic way.

◆ It provides a feeling of solidarity in that "most people" feel a certain way.

◆ It empowers or blesses a proposal, a course of action, or an individual or group.

The Cons:

◆ It may come across as decisions made by "them," "the organization," "city hall," or the "in crowd," to those who disagree.

◆ It may not notice or give credence to the silent majority that needs or wants to be heard.

◆ It may foster competitive decision-making.

The Minority Decision

A few individuals may sway a decision in their favor by forcing their will on the majority either by outspokenness or the use of threats. The outspokenness of a few at a school board meeting coupled with their threats to start calling the parents of school children to get their support may cause the board to reschedule morning bus pick-up for a later time. Or a minority of seniors may force the air conditioning to be set at a higher temperature in the church after several people complain that it aggravates their arthritis.

The Pros

- ◆ It avoids a win/lose or a lose/lose situation by trying to keep everyone happy.

- ◆ It attempts to be sensitive to individuals and minorities, and their needs, problems, and concerns.

- ◆ It helps separate some of the larger and smaller issues and allows for the participation of individuals and small interest groups.

The Cons:

- ◆ It may reflect a lack of leadership or an unwillingness to make the hard decisions.

- ◆ It may not foster the "common good" of the whole parish.

- ◆ It allows the "tail to wag the dog" by ceding power to those who make the most noise.

- ◆ It weakens or destroys the process or procedures that are in place for the orderly running of the parish.

The Consensus Decision

Many prefer this method of making decisions that will strongly impact the lives of the parishioners. Consensus means that every member of the board, committee, or group agrees with the overall thrust of the decision and will not stand in the way of its being implemented. This does not mean that each voting member agrees with every aspect of the proposal. However they can live with it, and can support their vote when challenged by others. Consensus decision-making is often very time consuming. Yet it also forces the group to come together to make the kind of decision they all can support.

The consensus model is usually preferred where opinions are divided and feelings are running deep. Here is a step-by-step process based on a consensus model developed by Thomas Sweetser and Carol Wisniewski Holden in *Leadership in a Successful Parish* that has been found to be effective for reaching a consensus decision:

1. Have everyone present make a commitmment to devote whatever time is necessary to reach a consensus.

2. Set aside a time for (quiet) prayer, asking God's help in the discerning process.

3. Select a facilitator from among the group who is best able to listen to each person's opinions and offer feedback to the group about the key areas of disagreement. It may not always be best to choose the chairperson for such a role.

4. Go around the group and have each person, without interruption, state briefly his or her opinion.

5. As this is taking place, everyone else is to jot down areas of agreement and disagreement.

6. With the help of the facilitator have the group focus on the points where there is disagreement. Then consider alternatives and options so that everyone in the group can eventually accept the proposal and feel good about the outcome. Sometimes a consensus can be reached by utilizing a trial period for a given proposal.

7. Once a consensus has been reached, it should be written down and clearly explained so that everyone in the group fully understands what has been decided. Often various members have different perceptions of what was decided. When the decision is later retold to others who were not at the meeting, overstatement or coloring can happen and hostility can result.

8. After a lengthy discernment period, if a consensus cannot be reached, a default decision may be the only alternative.

The consensus approach cannot and should not be used for every item. There is not enough time. Consensus is only used when a great deal of division and animosity is apt to result from a particular decision. Although very time-consuming it is well worth the effort for the unity it produces among the members of the group. To be successful, consensus requires the three "P's"—patience, practice, and prayer.

The Pros:

◆ It allows for a full discussion of the various sides of an issue or proposal.

◆ It avoids a win/lose situation and may result in a win/win decision.

◆ It fosters unity and solidarity among the group members.

◆ It provides discernment on a variety of issues under discussion.

The Cons:

◆ It is very time-consuming.

◆ It may avoid certain "hot" issues that still need to be dealt with.

◆ It may result in a decision that is vague or general.

◆ It may provide little or no direction when it is sorely needed.

◆ It may provide a lose/lose situation.

The Default Decision

This is one of the more popular ways decisions are made—by default! Many potentially good decisions are tabled by indecision or sent to some subcommittee to be put into limbo. A non-decision is still a decision.

Some matters that are potentially explosive and divisive are best handled by default. It is not a question of avoiding the issue, but rather of realizing that certain matters are win/lose or lose/lose situations. Living with the current situation is deemed better than making a change that will alienate certain people on the staff or in the congregation.

An example of this might be a liturgy committee or a parish council that on occasion is asked to deal with the disruption caused by children crying at Mass. Various solutions have been proposed and tried but with limited success. A more aggressive approach would only produce antagonisms as well as create a win/lose situation. After a considerable discussion of the implications and the fall-out from the proposal, the group decides they are in no position to make a decision.

The Pros:

◆ It allows the status-quo to continue.

◆ It avoids a win/lose or lose/lose situation.

◆ It hopes that the situation will resolve itself over time.

The Cons:

◆ It breeds frustration with groups or members who feel a decision is necessary.

◆ It allows certain situations or matters to worsen.

◆ It may mean that an issue or a situation that does not resolve itself will return again and again to the agenda.

Making Effective Decisions

Even when a decision is made after a lengthy struggle, a question that often lingers is: Was this an effective decision? Will it have an impact? Will it be divisive or unifying? Here are some suggestions to help make effective decisions.

1. Spend sufficient time going over the initial question until everyone agrees on what the real issue or problem is.

2. Get everyone to open up and to state their opinion.

3. Do not argue over various opinions. Try testing them out to see what they would mean or lead to if adopted.

4. Discuss how various opinions might be tested out.

5. Encourage dissenting opinions.

6. Keep an open mind. Try to hear the side of an issue that is different from your own.

7. Make compromises as the discussion proceeds.

8. Always consider alternatives. Is the decision necessary?

9. Build a process. This makes it easier to adapt or make changes in decisions.

Making a Motion

Many boards, committees, and groups in a church tend to be informal at their meetings and shy away from putting their proposals or issues in the form of a motion that is made, seconded, discussed, amended, and then voted on. Some may want to consider this process. It's a great help in facilitating regular meetings. Knowing exactly what is being decided upon during and after the meeting is important. Parish councils and school boards tend to be more formalized, but staff meetings and committee meetings may want to consider going this more formal route as well.

Handling Old Business

There can be a plethora of items to be addressed as old business and they are usually best left to the end of the meeting. This is the re-entry period, a time when the participants are coming down from any intensity surrounding major issues.

Old business items should be reviewed for progress or status and never be brought up to be rehashed. They are best handled by written summary reports that are distributed with the agenda before the meeting. This helps prevent old business items from developing into major issues at an upcoming meeting. It also limits the amount of time allowed for such matters and helps diffuse those folks who seem to get a second wind and renewed intensity when old business is introduced.

Handling New Business

New business items usually are introduced at the end of most meetings. Sometimes they point the way to serious consideration of an item for the next meeting's agenda. Weighty new business items should not be left for the end of the meeting, especially if a person or a group is awaiting an immediate answer or guidance on an issue. For example, the adult education committee has learned that a wonderful speaker is coming to a nearby parish and she can do a presentation in their parish the following week. Does the committee have the backing of the parish council to support it as a parishwide event so it can go ahead with its plans? This is new business that requires some discussion of parish policy. It may well be an item to be discussed earlier in the evening but with strict time limits.

New business should not be a litany of new items to be added to the agenda. These items need to be sorted through before the meeting with hopefully written summaries prepared and sent out. Ending the meeting on time is important to the integrity of the business being handled.

Closing the Meeting

Meetings need to be orchestrated to finish on time. When a meeting ends an hour or more past its scheduled time, the chairperson is no doubt anxious to conclude matters and get people on their way home. When a meeting is so tardy in ending, it disrupts the lives of many people.

Children and/or spouses are calling. Maintenance people are waiting to shut off lights and lock doors. Finishing on time allows the leader to conclude on a positive note, to thank everyone for their cooperation and their participation if the meeting went reasonably well.

If the meeting was difficult, the leader should strive for some words to help heal the hurts. This too can be aided through a closing prayer that is more than a quick pass at a familiar prayer. For example, suppose intense emotions were displayed at a meeting. The leader might try ending with a prayer such as:

> Lord, our emotions ran high tonight. I personally thank you for this. It tells me how much everyone really cares about our parish. I worry about the day when no one cares enough to be as passionately involved as people were tonight.
>
> I'm proud to be a part of this faith community, Lord. Although the air was heavy tonight and tempers flared, people treated one another with respect. No one was put down for what he or she believed. That shows we're trying to live up to the message of the Gospel. Thank you, God, and praise you. Amen.

An attempt should be made to close the meeting noting some positive accomplishment: "We've got a good sense of where we're going with our parish mission." It is frustrating to witness a group of people leave a meeting room muttering to themselves about hours of wasted time. Some important matters may well have been accomplished during the meeting, but it is not easy at times for the participants to recognize what the saving grace was. The positives need to be highlighted in the final summary or conclusion. For example:

In many ways this was a difficult meeting for all of us tonight. We heard some very strong voices against using a piano in church instead of the organ. There were some honest and straightforward comments that needed to be spoken. I feel we all grew tremendously in our knowledge and appreciation of all that goes into planning our liturgies and the selection of music as a result of an extremely well-done report and the discussion that followed. I believe we are all relieved that certain music will not be forced on us. On occasion the piano will be used with those hymns that are more prayerful and celebrative when they are accompanied by the piano. We give a strong vote of confidence to our fine liturgy director and to our devoted music director for the wonderful talents that they contribute to our parish.

If any decisions were reached, the chairperson should restate these in a clear and concise way. Assignments can be reiterated at this time. Even other issues that were informational, creative, or team-building should be summarized as to what was accomplished. Relating this to the larger goals of the parish or its vision and mission is also helpful.

The Closing Prayer

For many meetings the closing prayer might well be an important part of the agenda. It's an opportunity to put the meeting into a faith perspective. It's a chance for each person to look within. Usually it's beneficial if a member of the group prepares a closing prayer, one that is not too lengthy, but one that addresses the nature of the meeting. It should not sugar coat, nor should it be as somber or as silent as a wake. Spontaneous prayer might be appropriate, or a preplanned reading from scripture or from a spiritual writer may also bring the meeting to a meditative close.

Here's an example of a closing prayer:

> God, we felt your presence here in this room with us tonight, opening our minds and softening our hearts. It's because we love you so much and we cherish this parish community you've given us that we feel as strongly as we do. Just as our own families accept us, warts and all, so may this our parish family strive to do the same. May we now pray over our deliberations and our disagreements in the coming weeks to better see your will. And when we gather around your altar, may it be as one body in Jesus' name. Amen.

Often there is milling around that continues after a meeting. This is part of the re-entry process. But this is not a time to rehash the meeting or to discuss personalities who have been involved. It is either a time for follow-up on any assignments from the meeting or for socializing.

Four

Evaluating Your Meetings

"So *how do you think it went?" "Are we any fur-ther along?" "What were some of the underlying things we couldn't get at?"*

The time following a meeting is not just a time to give a sigh of relief and let what went on slip from one's mind. There is almost always a need to follow-up and follow through. But first an immediate debriefing should occur. Once the milling around has come to an end and the participants are about to leave, the chairperson can button-hole a member or two for feedback. Open questions like those above will provide immediate feedback. So often the chair-person or an individual member misinterprets or misunderstands some of what happened at the meeting. Sometimes issues are not put on the table for various reasons. A brief wrap-up for ten or fifteen minutes can point the way for what needs to happen now that the meeting is concluded.

Some Points for Consideration

Here are some points that often are considered after a meeting so that further action can be taken and the next meeting can build on what has hap-pened:

There Was Not Enough Time
to Treat the Subject Matter Properly

Even with the best-laid plans, a streamlined agenda, an able leader, and attentive participants, there simply may not be enough time to deal ade-quately with all the main items of the meeting.

The discussion may bring to light many more issues that beforehand were not known. Sometimes an hour or more goes by with the group concentrating on just one aspect of an issue. The discussion may lead to an impasse, not as a result of conflict, but of a quandary due to various unknowns. Because of the high degree of interdependence in parish and diocesan life, it is important for groups to think in terms of the entire parish or diocese. A pastoral council may be discussing the need for a pastoral associate, yet find itself in uncharted waters and at a stalemate due to diocesan rules and regulations. More information is often needed as well as more time at a subsequent meeting.

The Meeting Needs the Expertise of People Who Were Not Present

Sometimes the person whose counsel, expertise, or authority was needed before a decision could be made or a problem solved was not present. Perhaps the matter can be resolved by having the chairperson or a small subcommittee meet with this person.

People in a variety of positions and a host of ministries need to be consulted, informed, and give their approval as policies are made or shifted and decisions brought about. For example, a change in the Mass schedule will affect a multitude of people, ranging from the maintenance staff, the secretary who answers the phone, the ministers who serve at the liturgy, as well as neighboring parishes. This is necessary work that needs to be done apart from the meeting itself.

Additional Time for Assessment Is Needed

Policies and decisions that cause change in the way things have been done for years in the church affect a lot of people. And most people are sensitive to change. Once a matter is out on the table and dealt with, the participants and the leader need time to assess the subject and discuss it with others. They may want to consult and see how a similar matter was handled in another parish. This time for assessment need not go on for many months, but for matters that are new or unsettling the additional time may be well spent.

Dealing with Fallout from a Meeting

Sometimes an unpopular decision or a policy change has to be made and this leads to hostility after the meeting. There are no easy solutions to dealing with this, but clear communication that includes giving the reasons for the decision is important. The timeliness of such communication is vital. Getting a letter out the next morning to all the school parents, having the pastor and/or the parish council president address the congregation the following weekend, or calling a staff meeting immediately afterwards are sometimes necessary. The information should be presented in a straightforward and concise manner. It is vital to give people in today's church all the information they need.

If there is appreciable dissent from a committee decision it is best to meet it head on early, well, and effectively. One possibility is to have the committee meet with those who are objecting. This might be arranged after a Mass on Sunday. As difficult as this might seem, this is an effective way of diffusing a potential problem, since most dissenters will likely attend.

People need a place and a time when they can be heard. This will not be the first time in their lives a decision or a policy went against their wishes and they'll welcome the opportunity to be heard. And it may lead to some constructive suggestions.

Use a Task Force to Resolve an Issue

In reflecting on what happened or did not happen at the meeting, it sometimes becomes evident that further meeting time is not the best way to make progress. Additional discussion time would not be useful. For whatever reason, this group can take the matter no further. Appointing a task force to address the issue and bring the matter to a resolution is often effective. A task force is an ad hoc group that works for a limited time to accomplish a given task in a certain manner and is commissioned to report back to the committee by an appointed date. This is done at the discretion of the leader or whoever is in charge.

A task force is able to engage the talents and the abilities of additional parishioners. And while standing groups and committees exist often with no clear accomplishments, task forces can provide visible outcomes. Participants feel they have done something useful. New leaders may emerge as a result of being invited to participate and serve.

Following Up and Following Through

The real benefit of a meeting happens afterward as the participants go about gathering resources and information, communicating with others, getting out letters of appreciation and congratulation, as well as getting the policies or the decisions into the main stream of the parish, school, or diocese. The tendency after a meeting is to let matters drop, at least for a week or two or until the next meeting is in sight. This is not an effective way to carry on business. When the business and the resolutions of the meeting fall flat immediately afterward, most of the energy of the meeting is lost.

The follow-up and the follow through should begin within a day or two after the meeting. This may be too much for the leader or chairperson to handle so another member of the group can assist. This may be a good way to help train or empower someone to take the leader's position in the future. People who need to be contacted can now be reached by many means: phone, fax, mail, or e-mail.

All too often someone with an important assignment is left hanging without any contact, interest, or support from the leader until the day before the next meeting. People need support and nurturing to do assignments, especially those for which they receive no pay.

Lack of support usually results in the assignment not being completed or being done unsatisfactorily. This may not necessarily be the member's fault. In the maze of the discussion at the meeting, the participant's exact responsibility may not have been made clear.

Nothing Changes as a Result of Meetings

We have all heard it said, "We've been talking about the same things for the last year, and nothing has changed as result of all these meetings." This kind of statement reflects a despair that leads to a disdain for meetings. People come to expect that meetings are merely all talk, and that those in authority will keep it that way. There may be more than an element of truth in such a statement.

What people need to see is visible output from their efforts. If not, then they become discouraged and frustrated. They ultimately vent their frustrations through disruptive tactics or by circumventing the various organized meetings in the parish. The best intentioned, best conducted meeting serves little purpose if no action results. If action does follow, but is not monitored and reported back to the original participants, they too will be frustrated. It is the responsibility of the leaders of the parish and of the diocese to provide the structures and the training necessary to have meetings that work.

Five

Listening with Understanding

A *key element of parish meetings that work is listening. So much of what is said may well be heard, but not understood. Hearing is one thing, listening and understanding is another.*

The leader may walk out of a meeting feeling good that the agenda was handled reasonably well. Items were discussed, voted on, and the meeting ended close to the appointed hour.

Others at the same meeting may walk out feeling poorly because they feel many of the real issues were not dealt with, some important items were glossed over, and a number of valid points and suggestions were never highlighted for further consideration or discussion.

What to Be Listening for . . . Overcoming the Barriers

Before a given meeting, the leader and another person or two from the board, possibly the pastor or the principal, might benefit from discussing the goals of the upcoming meeting and what the leader should be listening for so that the purpose of the meeting is achieved.

The following checklist is helpful for the leader to go over before a scheduled meeting so as to provide the proper atmosphere for listening.

♦ I want the meeting to focus on those issues and problems that are important to our parish and to those coming to the meeting.

♦ I want those who are attending to speak up and speak frankly about what is on their mind and how they view a particular issue.

♦ I want the members of the group to come up with as much information as they can and to look at the issues from a variety of viewpoints.

♦ I want those who are coming to the meeting to get a greater understanding and insight into the problems as they are being discussed.

♦ I want those in the group to get a handle on the "bigger picture" and how what is going to be discussed fits into the whole parish and community as well as the larger church.

♦ I want those who are attending to get at the deeper causes of the problems as they surface.

♦ I want the members of the group to focus on a possible direction to be taken and viable solutions as different members speak and listening takes place.

♦ I want any difficult and sensitive areas to be brought to light, identified, and hopefully resolved in a spirit of openness and honesty.

Listening to What Is Being Said

The leader of the meeting as well as those who participate need to ask themselves—"Am I really listening to what is being said?" Here are three checkpoints to see if this is happening:

1. Is the whole problem being considered?

2. What in my background or experience is helping me to fully comprehend what is being discussed?

3. Is the discussion centering around the symptoms rather than the causes of the problem?

When a person is not "actively listening," that is, paying attention to both the vocal and the non-verbal messages that are being given, then the majority of what is being communicated is missed. A lack of listening is a major barrier to understanding.

Barriers to Listening

Dr. Ralph Nichols, a professor of anthropology at the University of Chicago, says that not listening can be classified into specific habits that a person develops throughout life. Here are Dr. Nichols' eight habits of poor listeners, their causes, and what can be done to get rid of the habits. Looking over this list will prove helpful to both the leader and the members. It will help everyone to consider what habits they have picked up and what can be done to "kick the habit."

1. The In-out Listener

The Cause: Most people think four times faster than the average person speaks.

To Correct: Write down whatever you were thinking about that caused you to stop listening. This will help you to recall what you were thinking about at the time. You will stop worrying about forgetting it. It is important to get back to listening.

2. The Red Flag Listener

The Cause: Some words upset us when we hear them, and we stop thinking: for example, "hierarchy," "accountability," "discernment."

To Correct: Write the word down, then listen. Is the speaker using the word correctly or adding a new meaning?

3. The Closed-minded Listener

The Cause: There is no reason to listen because we will hear nothing new.

To Correct: Set a goal to actually listen to see if the person talking is saying anything new. This will force you to listen.

4. The Day-dreaming Listener

The Cause: A word or an idea comes up that causes us to think of something else.

To Correct: If you find your mind is wandering during the meeting, jot the thoughts down and then start listening.

5. The Too Technical/Complex Listener

The Cause: You may be sitting there thinking the subject is too technical or complex for you to understand.

To Correct: If you spot a subject on the agenda before the meeting that is unfamiliar to you, seek out information on it. At the meeting, follow the discussion and ask questions. You are probably not the only one in the dark.

6. The Mind-guarding Listener

The Cause: You may not want your pet idea or point of view challenged. You stop listening, become defensive, and even plan a counter-attack.

To Correct: Work to understand what the speaker has to say. Get the other side of the issue. This leads to better understanding and enables you to reply in a calm and reasonable manner.

7. The Court-reporter Listener

The Cause: You try to take extensive and detailed notes, only the speaker talks faster than you can write.

To Correct: Jot down the key words. Later put them in an outline format.

8. The Hubbub Listener

The Cause: The distractions that happen at the meeting, like noises from another room.

To Correct: Practice tuning out the distractions and concentrating on what the speaker is saying.

The Leader as Listener

The secret of good listening is concentrating on what is being said and trying not to think about how to respond. The leader of the meeting is in a strategic position to listen at the meeting. Active and effective listening on the part of the leader will go a long way in making the meeting work. Here are some tips on how to become a more effective listener:

♦ Paraphrase what the speaker has said: "Oh, so

you believe that. . . ." Or, "Based on what you've said, I realize that you want to. . . ."

◆ Maintain good eye contact. When the leader or a group member is shuffling through notes or looking around the room, it sends a message that the speaker or the message is not important.

◆ Nod your head to the one speaking when this is appropriate. It is a sign of affirmation and it says the speaker is being heard.

◆ Allow enough time to cover an important topic on the agenda. Adjust the agenda as needed. Listening does take time.

◆ When silence happens, let it be. Silence is a time to reflect.

◆ Try to get beyond the symptoms of the problem to highlight the problem itself and its causes.

◆ Assist the speaker and the other participants at the meeting to associate the problem with the causes.

◆ Invite and encourage the speaker and the other members to develop an action plan for solving the problem.

◆ Keep to the subject matter at hand.

◆ Show interest in the issues and in those people who are addressing them.

◆ Be on the lookout for the non-verbal signs as

they surface: side comments, crossed arms, slouching, facial expressions, and so on. These provide the clues to where the group is at and what to take as the next step.

◆ Be understanding, even when this is difficult. Don't interrupt unless necessary.

◆ Show empathy by not jumping to conclusions or giving advice when it is not warranted.

◆ Summarize the discussion as it proceeds and at the end of the discussion.

The Right Question

Another helpful way to become a more effective listener is to ask the right questions as the discussion takes place. Use of the following questions will not only deepen the level of communication, it will also help reduce the chances of conflict:

◆ Disarming questions: "Do you think I can help you solve this problem?"

◆ Bridge-building questions: "I'd like to help you. Why don't we try to solve this problem together?"

◆ Questions that foster understanding: "I'm sure you have good reasons for thinking the way you do. Won't you share them?"

◆ Truth-revealing questions: "You seem to be well-informed. Where and when did you get your information?"

◆ Tolerance-producing questions: "I still see

another side to this. May I share my thoughts on this with you?"

◆ Questions that point up disadvantages: "Do you see any dangers that could arise if we followed your suggestions?"

◆ Questions that put another in your shoes: "What would you do if you were in my position?"

◆ Questions that can lead to a compromise: "What do you see are the alternatives? Are there any other opinions?"

◆ Questions that ask for time: "We will need time to re-examine all this. Can we get together soon to explore various solutions?"

We all have an innate sense that appreciates when someone really listens to us. Such moments are important and cherished. Reading the reaction of a group will require the leader and fellow participants to listen with understanding. The ability to react to someone's words and vocal intonation will greatly benefit the group as well as adjust the direction of the meeting.

Developing good listening habits helps leaders and members maintain motivation and interest and usually results in productive meetings. It's a skill people appreciate.

Six

Some Final Notes

What would happen if the leader scheduled a meeting and no one came? Without participants, there is no need for a leader, an agenda, a meeting room, or someone to take minutes. Participants make the meeting.

The responsibility of a participant, however, is far more than just showing up. The success of the meeting depends on the preparation, the resources, the skills, the commitment, the creativity, the enthusiasm, and the active participation of every person on the board, committee, council, or group.

Preparing for a Meeting

It is of crucial importance that each member of a committee, council, or group prepare well for upcoming meetings. At the very least, they need to know what is expected of them for the specific topics that are to be discussed. If participants have not received an agenda when notified about the meeting, then they need to make a call to the chairperson or someone on the committee to get one or to at least find out what will be happening.

Participants should go further in their personal preparation by conducting additional research into issues and problems to be discussed so that they can come to the meeting prepared to offer stimulating, well-founded views. Often the participant is a member of a ministry in the parish or represents a given group. Soliciting a variety of opinions from these sources to carry to the meeting is important. This is better than "building a case" for or against an issue and coming to the meeting prepared to "win." The goal is always what is best for the parish, the school, or the diocese and not to win or lose on an issue. Parish life and ministry is not about winning and losing, but about serving.

An active committee member is on the alert for information and perspectives that can help the committee achieve its goals and to make parish life better. It's important that participants not tune out once the meeting is over and not turn on again until the next meeting. Often enough the kind of information the committee needs comes to the forefront when the committee is not in session. A responsible member is alert, sensitive to, and even in pursuit of information the committee might need. This means follow-up and follow-through. But it leads to a much greater participation and a more fruitful meeting. One parish committee talked about purchasing window shades for the auditorium on and off for many months. When a member finally did some follow-up and follow-through, a decision could finally be made and the shades were bought and installed.

Becoming a Member of the Group

There are several ways for someone to become a member of a board, a committee, or a group. This may happen through election, selection, or de facto by a position one holds in the parish, school, or diocese. A member of the pastoral council or the school board may be elected by the parish in a general election. Some parishes effectively use a selection process whereby the parish-at-large nominates candidates and a selection committee then interviews the various nominees. The selection committee then chooses members who possess the skills that are needed and whom they believe will contribute the most. A pastor, a principal, or a bishop may choose committee members who they feel are best suited for the task. The chairperson may do the same.

Almost all of the members of committees, councils, and groups are volunteers with many other full-time commitments. Most people come to serve both as a result of a sense of duty and being buttoned-holed into it. An active and a full participant must get far beyond being drafted to serve. He or she must truly take ownership. Participants are major stakeholders in the parish. How successful the parish will be following Jesus' example in reaching out to others rests on how effective the structures are and how active the participants become. The mission of the church is hardly served by a passive member who goes to listen and occasionally to add a comment or two with no real commitment to the process or the final outcome of the meeting.

How to Be a Responsible Participant

There are a number of ways for participants at meetings to be responsible. There is a time to talk and a time to listen carefully; a time to challenge, and a time to hold back; a time to disagree and a time to hold one's tongue; a time to be forceful and a time to be humble; a time to volunteer and a time to sit on one's hands. Let's consider a few of the practical ways in which a participant can act responsibly.

Be Organized When Contributing

The old adage "Think before you speak" fits well here. In an active discussion the participant needs to actively listen and not just wait to interject her or his comments whether or not they are relevant to the issue at that moment. Insightful contributions are needed, not rehashing of what was said ten minutes earlier. Clear thinking expressed in an unambiguous way is always welcomed. Thoughts are always best expressed when first jotted down as notes and compressed into a simple, basic idea or two.

If a participant has a report to give at the meeting, a summary of the report is best submitted in writing before the meeting. A summary is almost always better than a full report because members do not have time to read a stack of full reports before a meeting. Full reports that are presented verbally are one of the greatest wastes of time at meetings. If the group needs to take action as a result of the report, they have had a few days to digest it and they already have it in their hands. The author of the report can answer questions at the meeting and guide the group along.

Making One Point at a Time

When some people get the floor they evidently feel it will be their only opportunity so they touch on a number of items. This only invites other group members to wander in many different directions as well. People then begin responding to a whole host of comments and issues being raised. It is best to present one coherent point at a time. It takes a great deal of restraint not to make a jumble of reactions to someone else's comments.

Nonverbals Say a Lot

When we observe body language and study facial expressions of those who come to meetings, we discover a broad range of messages that are being transmitted, from attention and interest to complete boredom and hostility. They speak volumes about what is or is not happening in a meeting, especially at critical points or as a meeting wears on. A responsible participant should try to portray a positive facial response and a body posture that demonstrates participation and interest.

Bring Along Meeting Manners

Your meeting manners should be as good as they are at work or important social events. Respect the views of others. People are entitled to their opinions. Don't read reports or shuffle papers when others are talking. Don't chat with someone while a presentation is being made. It's distracting and displays a lack of respect to others in the room.

Once a person has accepted the invitation to serve on a board, committee, or council, then a degree of group loyalty should follow. It is not wise to criticize the group or the decisions it makes outside of the group. Matters discussed and other things that happen at most meetings are confidential and should be treated in such a manner. If you have difficulty with a group or the policies it makes, take it up with members of the group privately. Or simply sit down and discuss what is causing the turmoil. This may point the way to some well needed self-examination or might well lead the group to reflect on how it does its business. It is possible that being a member of this group is not where your talents can be best utilized.

It is important to help the chairperson whenever possible. Many leaders simply have a difficult job to do. Too many participants leave it up to the leader to deal with difficult members. And leaders have a sense of relief when someone other than themselves raises the hard questions. And finally, you greatly aid the meeting process when you arrive on time, are prepared, and observe the guidelines and the ground rules that have been set.

Appreciating the Uniqueness of Each Group

Almost all of what has been presented so far applies to just about every board, council, committee, and group that conducts meetings in a parish or a diocese. Yet each group has its own identity, mood, flavor, and style for conducting business and attaining its goals. The different culture and style of a parish or the many different styles within a parish naturally determine the way a meeting is held: the procedures used, the time scheduling, the degree of formality, and so on. Some groups are more formal than others. On pastoral councils or school boards, there is an element of rank, with a president, vice-president, secretary, and treasurer. A staff, a pastoral team, a committee, or a group of teachers may function more interdependently, planning together, sharing insights and responsibilities, and meeting on a regular basis to coordinate their efforts.

An ongoing level of frustration attached to meetings should be looked into in light of the information and processes presented here. A committee meeting may or may not need to have minutes taken. It may function adequately with a leader who summarizes as she or he goes along. It certainly needs to begin on time and have follow-up and follow through on any action items.

How Long? . . . How Often a Meeting?

Both of these questions are asked and answered by each group. Most parish meetings in the evening begin at 7:00 or 7:30pm and last for about two hours. Once a meeting runs much beyond two hours, little is accomplished.

More and more committee meetings are being scheduled for about an hour in the morning before work. Some people have rather flexible schedules and can attend a meeting during the daytime or on a Saturday. Many have found that an early morning or a daytime meeting is more productive and progresses more smoothly since there are built-in time limits and people are not as tired as they are at the end of the day.

How often a group meets is determined by the group's responsibilities. At times it is good to cancel a meeting for the reasons that were given earlier in this book. Breaks in the calendar are a matter for the group to discuss. Some groups tend to lose their momentum with summer breaks and holiday respites. If weekly meetings become burdensome, consider holding them bi-weekly especially if these are staff meetings. People need to feel they are taking care of their normal work load and a weekly meeting is a potential burden.

Using Robert's Rules of Order

The standard procedures for conducting meetings can be found in a book entitled, *Robert's Rules of Order.* Its use may not be necessary for most parish meetings, but a familiarity with the book is advantageous for anyone running or participating in more formal meetings. It contains much helpful data on procedures, such as making motions and conducting a meeting with order and integrity.

When the Person with the Most Authority Is Not the Leader

When the person with the most authority is not the leader or the chairperson, it is good for the chairperson to discuss with him or her what role he or she will play. This situation may arise on a pastoral council or a school board where the pastor or the principal is a member.

The chairperson has the responsibility of conducting the meeting according to an agreed upon set of guidelines and ground rules and should not be intimidated by the presence of "authorities" in the group. Nor should the chairperson continually turn to them for guidance or direction. If the person in authority is unduly silent in discussions or on the other hand is forever interjecting comments, then the chairperson is well advised to discuss this with him or her after the meeting. It may require a strong stand indicating that the one in authority has to abide by the same procedures as everyone else if the meeting is to be productive.

Some social time involving the person in authority and the chairperson as well as members of the group can help such a situation. Everyone needs to feel relaxed at meetings and in discussions rather than intimidated.

Developing a
Wider Perspective on Meetings

The aim of this book has been to assist those who regularly attend church-related meetings and who are involved in group process through boards, committees, and councils. So often the goals of these groups, such as starting a young adult ministry or getting the parents of children in religious education to become more involved, is established. Yet the means to achieving that goal, namely, an effectively run deliberation and decision-making process, is never attended to or examined.

If the process by which meetings are conducted is not structured and well planned, then the most noble goals will not be attained. This process can be improved through preparation and the application of selected techniques that have been found to be effective. Problems will get solved, decisions will be made, and a sense of ownership will ensue. This will actually lead people to look forward to meetings. Inertia will cease and a sense of accomplishment prevail.

At times the personality of a member or two of the group is blamed for many of the problems that take place. A participant may talk a lot or have a chip on his or her shoulder. Surely, personalities play a role in the success of a meeting. Yet, in the long run, the committee and board process makes for success or failure. If the process is good and it works, then trust the process! Blaming one or two people on the committee is like blaming one person on an assembly line for a car that is not performing properly. That's only part of the problem.

We also need to take a look at the role of the leader to see if it is a well defined role and if he or she is effectively carrying out that role. Then we should look at the roles of the participants to see if they are also clear and if members understand how they are to function on the committee. Once the roles and the responsibilities have been clarified and put into place, meetings will run much more smoothly and the jobs will get done.

Improving parish meetings to make them work begins before the meeting ever takes place. The meeting is only the tip of the iceberg. The "before and after" parts are the infrastructure that make for a successful meeting. The meeting is the public display of all the work and energy that has gone on to get to the point of the meeting.

All too often our church is not planning-oriented. It often waits for a crisis to develop before acting. "Let's play it by ear" is an underlying attitude that often prevails. But playing it by ear results in confusion, lack of information, poor communication, and in the end, frustration and even hostility.

Good planning and preparation, so that people know what to expect and can prepare themselves, decreases the likelihood of making poor decisions. It also helps prevent meetings that seem to go nowhere. Time for feedback, creative brainstorming, and team-building is energizing time in the life of any board, committee, or group. It is time for the discussion to be free-flowing. From meetings run this way can come a whole new vision for a parish, a school, a diocese, or an organization.

Even conflict at meetings can be useful to a degree. It at least shows that people are interested and are taking a stand on the issues. But conflict needs to be managed effectively so it does not become the primary focus of the meeting. The structure of the agenda becomes an effective way of managing tensions that arise.

Because the demands for ministry and service from the church are increasing and the church's traditional resources are diminishing, the need for group problem-solving and group decision-making is ever increasing. As the challenges and the problems become more complex, different types of knowledge and skills will be required. This too will increase the need for group decision-making. And finally, since ministry and the building up of the kingdom is the work of many hands and hearts and not the task of a single pair of hands or an individual heart, the owners of those hands and hearts by coming together form a community in a true sense of the word, become the church, the people of the God, the Body of Christ.

Resources Used in This Book

Walter M. Abbott and Joseph Gallagher, eds., *The Documents of Vatican II* (New York: Herder and Herder, Association Press, 1966).

Canon Law Society of Great Britain and Ireland, *The Code of Canon Law in English Translation* (London: Collins, 1983).

Robert G. Howes, *Parish Planning, A Practical Guide to Shared Responsibility* (Collegeville, MN: The Liturgical Press, 1994).

Pamela J. Newman, Ph.D. and Alfred F. Lynch, *Behind Closed Doors: A Guide to Successful Meetings* (Englewood Cliffs, NJ: Prentice-Hall, Inc., 1983).

Thomas Sweetser and Carol Wisniewski Holden, *Leadership in a Successful Parish* (San Francisco, CA: Harper Row, 1987).

Robert H. Waterman, *The Renewal Factor* (New York: Bantam Books, 1987).

George M. Williams, *Improving Parish Management* (Mystic, CT: Twenty-Third Publications, 1983).